Ruth Henig	The Origins of the First World War
Ruth Henig	The Origins of the Second World War 1933–1939
Ruth Henig	Versailles and After: Europe 1919–1933
P.D. King	Charlemagne
Stephen J. Lee	Peter the Great
Stephen J. Lee	The Thirty Years War
J.M. MacKenzie	The Partition of Africa 1880–1900
Michael Mullett	Calvin
Michael Mullett	The Counter-Reformation
Michael Mullett	James II and English Politics 1678–1688
Michael Mullett	Luther
David Newcombe	Henry VIII and the English Reformation
Robert Pearce	Attlee's Labour Governments 1945–51
Gordon Phillips	The Rise of the Labour Party 1893–1931
J.H. Shennan	International Relations in Europe 1689–1789
J.H. Shennan	Louis XIV
Margaret Shennan	The Rise of Brandenburg–Prussia
David Shotter	Augustus Caesar
David Shotter	The Fall of the Roman Republic
David Shotter	Tiberius Caesar
Keith J. Stringer	The Reign of Stephen
John K. Walton	Disraeli
John K. Walton	The Second Reform Act
Michael J. Winstanley	Gladstone and the Liberal Party
Michael J. Winstanley	Ireland and the Land Question 1800–1922
Alan Wood	The Origins of the Russian Revolution 1861–1917
Alan Wood	Stalin and Stalinism
Austin Woolrych	England Without a King 1649–1660

LANCASTER PAMPHLETS

France Before the Revolution

Second Edition

J.H. Shennan

London and New York

First published 1983
by Methuen & Co. Ltd
11 New Fetter Lane, London EC4P 4EE

Second edition published 1995
by Routledge
11 Fetter Lane, London EC4P 4EE

Simultaneously published in the USA and Canada
by Routledge
29 West 35th Street, New York, NY 10001

Typeset in Bembo by
Ponting–Green Publishing Services, Chesham, Bucks
Printed and bound in Great Britain by
Clays Ltd, St Ives PLC

British Library Cataloguing in Publication Data
Shennan, J.H.
France before the Revolution – 2Ed.
(Lancaster Pamphlets)
I. Title   II. Series
944.034

Library of Congress Cataloguing in Publication Data
Shennan, J. H.
France before the Revolution / J.H. Shennan. – 2nd ed.
p.   cm. – (Lancaster Pamphlets)
Includes bibliographical references.
1. France–History–Louis XV, 1715–1774.
2. France–History–Louis XVI, 1774–1793.
3. France–History–Revolution, 1789–1799–Causes.
I. Title.   II. Series.
DC131.S47   1995
944'.034–dc20   94-45999

ISBN 0–415–11945–6

Contents

Foreword

Lancaster Pamphlets offer concise and up-to-date accounts of major historical topics, primarily for the help of students preparing for Advanced Level examinations, though they should also be of value to those pursuing introductory courses in universities and other institutions of higher education. Without being all-embracing, their aims are to bring some of the central themes or problems confronting students and teachers into sharper focus than the textbook writer can hope to do; to provide the reader with some of the results of recent research which the textbook may not embody; and to stimulate thought about the whole interpretation of the topic under discussion.

Preface to the Second Edition

Since the first appearance of *France before the Revolution* in 1983 the bicentenary of the French Revolution has been celebrated. In order to make contemporary sense of that momentous and dramatic event, historians have re-examined the world of eighteenth-century France. This enlarged second edition takes account of this and of other historical work produced during the last decade. In particular it elaborates one of the themes signalled in the first edition: how the changing perception of government, from one of dynastic, divine-right kingship towards the idea of a national enterprise, first altered the relationship between the crown and the privileged orders, and ultimately undermined the old regime.

J.H. Shennan

1
Introduction

This pamphlet is primarily concerned with the years between 1715 and 1789, from the accession of Louis XV to the outbreak of the French Revolution. Because this period ends so dramatically it is difficult for historians to write about the eighteenth century without linking their work, directly or implicitly, to the events following 1789. It is tempting, in other words, to interpret eighteenth-century French history as a preparation for the Revolution. It was such a momentous event that it has always seemed a natural stopping and starting point, not only for historians but even for those who lived through the Revolution. The phrase *ancien régime*, or old order, which we commonly use to describe the organization of government and society before 1789 was only coined at about that time by men who were in the process of establishing a new kind of system. They looked back across the revolutionary divide in order to define the eighteenth century in terms of their own experience. It is understandable that historians, whose additional hindsight makes them even more conscious of the importance of the Revolution, might follow their example and write the history of the eighteenth century backwards, as it were, from the standpoint of 1789. The temptation to do so has recently been that much greater, with the celebration of the Revolution's bicentenary producing a spate of commemorative reassessments. However, we should remember that the men and women

1

who lived in France during Louis XV's reign (1715–74) and much of that of his successor, Louis XVI, had no inkling of approaching revolution and no means of understanding what that upheaval would involve. Like all of us they lived in the present and were powerless to foresee the future. The historian has some obligation, therefore, to write their history in such a way as to reflect their own understanding of events, circumstances and personalities, and not to subject them constantly to the distorting mirror of the French Revolution. Equally, for they do have the advantage of knowing what happened late in the century, historians must try to assess the extent to which the Revolution was caused by deep-seated problems as against the circumstances arising shortly before 1789.

Consideration of that important question requires the historian to take a view about fundamental changes, and accompanying stresses, which were affecting the French state not only during the eighteenth century but even earlier, during the long reign of Louis XIV (1643–1715). The argument that Louis defeated the power of the French nobility and established a centralized, absolutist state has been subjected to a good deal of historical revision. It now appears that the king drew heavily upon the support of the nobility in his policy of stabilizing and strengthening the state. The key feature of that policy was his ability to attract to himself, as the embodiment of the French state, the loyalty of all his subjects. He succeeded thereby in replacing the various bonds of patron–client loyalty which had previously empowered the nobility, without losing the latter's support. This was a significant achievement. By reasserting the great nobility's personal relationship with the crown, most visibly and symbolically at Versailles, Louis succeeded, paradoxically, in establishing the idea of universal loyalty to an impersonal national enterprise rather than to a dynasty. By extension a similar relationship grew up between the king and his chief advisers, members of the *noblesse de robe*, most of whose families had achieved their noble status through the acquisition of high office. These men depended for their continuing status more on the quality of their service to the crown than upon ancient lineage. Yet despite the increasingly professional nature of their role, Louis continued to view his ministers of state, whom he called to sit at his High Council, as loyal personal servants to whom he in turn showed loyalty. Only

2

seventeen ministers were appointed throughout the whole of the king's majority (1661–1715), most of them from one of three families, the Colbert, the Le Tellier and the Phélypeaux.

However, this reformulation of royal authority, based upon the medieval tradition of the *Curia Regis* or King's Court, which was intended to extend the power of the king's government in the early modern period, was not without its dangers for the crown. It was impossible for Louis XIV to increase his administrative control over the kingdom merely by extending the range of his personal intervention. That intervention was increasingly exercised on his behalf by agents: ministers, secretaries of state, intendants, all of whom were served by a growing army of expert advisers and clerks. This impersonal state machine which was thus in the process of formation would at some stage require some other justification than that traditionally associated with dynastic divine-right monarchy. It would demand a commitment to the state by all the subjects, based upon the equality of their responsibilities. Yet Louis's regime supported a society of orders which was characterized by a gross inequality of status and obligation between various groups. The nobility, for example, was accustomed to enjoying exemption from the burden of direct taxation. This contradiction came increasingly to weaken the government during the eighteenth century. In the words of an American historian, writing recently on this subject, 'The simultaneously personal and impersonal character of the "absolute" monarchy set the stage for the critical argument over public accountability in the last decade of the old regime'.[1] By the same token, in a world of large-scale warfare in which the government was forced to make increasingly heavy financial demands upon the subjects, social inequalities militated against the emergence of a patriotic spirit which was the natural concomitant of impersonal statehood.

When Louis XIV's great-grandson, Louis XV, ascended the throne in 1715 old loyalties and beliefs seemed still to be in the ascendant, but under the surface of the body politic subtle shifts and pressures were at work which would have long-term effects. Before examining them further, however, we must try to understand the nature of the old order, as it appeared to most observers on the morrow of Louis XIV's death.

2
The old order

The crown

The crown was the lynch-pin of the system providing the sole source of political authority in the state. French kings have been described as absolute rulers, and it is important to be clear about what that phrase means. It does not mean that the king could ride roughshod over the liberties of his subjects. Even in those areas of public policy where the king's authority had ultimately to prevail, for example in matters relating to the security of the realm, it was expected that he would take steps to reconcile the subjects' liberties with the royal prerogative. If war put the realm at risk and the king required additional exceptional revenue from taxation to cope with the danger, he would have to consult with the relevant groups, large and small, provincial estates, municipal assemblies, even the theologians of the Sorbonne, in order to justify his proposals. Beyond those public boundaries, all subjects remained free under the law which it was the king's duty to maintain; the alternative would have been a regime of slavery. A recent commentator, Nicholas Henshall, has suggested that the sense of individual freedom felt by all the subjects of the king of France reduces the significance usually ascribed to the possession of corporate rights.[2] However, that is to conflate private with public rights; the crown had a direct interest in the latter but not in the former.

4

As absolute rulers French kings were not limited in the execution of their powers by any other individuals, groups or institutions within their realm. Thus they were not directly accountable to their subjects for the manner in which they ruled. This did not mean however that their power was despotic, for that would have implied a refusal to recognize that their subjects possessed private and public rights. The French themselves made a clear distinction between absolute and despotic rule and it was the basis on which the king of France founded his authority which made the decisive difference. This basis was two-fold: the support of the law and of God. The order of succession to the French crown was governed by a principle which was considered so essential to the survival of the state that it was called a fundamental law. It stipulated that the heir to the throne would always be the eldest legitimate male relative in the direct line of descent from the previous ruler. Thus the king was always the legal source of authority in his realm, and was bound to take its laws seriously. A despotic ruler, on the other hand, would have felt no obligation to tolerate such restrictions upon his freedom of action. The fundamental law of succession was the starting point in the development of a strong judicial tradition in French government, centred upon the crown. Over the centuries the country's internal stability was secured through the exercise of the king's authority as chief judge, responsible for maintaining law and order and preserving the various rights of his subjects. His credibility as the political leader of France was inextricably linked with his role as guar-antor of a just regime. Originally the king had exercised author-ity directly through the *Curia Regis*, but with the passing of time he worked increasingly through his council, an organization which became more elaborate as the king became more de-pendent upon its members for expert advice. He also delegated his authority as judge to a hierarchy of law-courts, which included at the highest level the so-called sovereign courts, those great legal institutions, like the parlement of Paris, which heard cases on appeal from lower tribunals. As we shall see these bodies played an important political role during the eighteenth century. They were also the repositories of private law which, as the guarantor of a secure and just regime, it was the crown's task to support and maintain.

To add support to his position the king of France emphasized his special relationship with God. At his coronation each king was anointed with sacred oils and, with the title of His Most Christian Majesty, became God's representative in France, ruler by divine right. In that capacity he had to promote respect for Christian virtues and the divine commandments. If he neglected to do so he would have to answer to God after death for his failure. In a deeply religious age such a prospect was not to be taken lightly so that this spiritual support, while adding significantly to royal power and prestige, further reduced the dangers of royal despotism.

There are two other aspects of the monarch's relationship with his subjects which we must also take into account if we are fully to understand the crown's unique position under the old regime. First, as the highest nobleman in the land, the king was the natural leader of society. He gave significance and coherence to the social hierarchy established beneath him, a fact which further assisted the maintenance of a united kingdom. Secondly, because the subjects did not relate to the king as equal individuals but as part of a variety of corporate groups possessing different rights, the only source of national identity was the crown. Once again, therefore, we observe its importance as a unifying agent, the necessary common factor for all these different groups. The broadest division of French society, concealing a large number of sub-divisions, was by estate or order, and it is to the three estates of the realm that we now turn.

The estates of the realm

The first estate

The clergy constituted the first estate. So long as the population retained its keen awareness of the choice between eternal salvation and damnation in the next life, the prestige of the first estate was assured, for the church alone provided the means to salvation. During the eighteenth century ideas hostile to organized religion were propounded by writers of the French Enlightenment, and towards the end of the century there were signs in some quarters of doubts about the church's mission: vocations to the religious life diminished and so did the number of books and pamphlets on religious subjects. Also the long-running dispute between those ascetic French Catholics called

Jansenists (after Bishop Jansen, whose theological beliefs they supported) and the Order of Jesus, or Jesuits, who disapproved of the Jansenists' theological position and supported the Pope's right to condemn them, had troubled and increasingly discredited the French church since before Louis XIV's death. Yet it would be quite wrong to imply a widespread loss of faith in the country as a whole. The *curé*, or parish priest, remained a key figure both as the spiritual adviser to his flock and, in more immediately practical terms, as one of the most influential figures in his locality, responsible for assisting the sick and the needy. At the highest level the king retained his aura of divine right under the spiritual guidance of his father confessor, though clerics no longer dominated the royal administration. Nevertheless cardinals, archbishops and bishops remained leading public figures, and some like Cardinal Fleury (1653–1743) and Loménie de Brienne (1727–94) played very important roles in the government of eighteenth-century France.

Although *curés* on the one hand and cardinals on the other shared membership of the first estate, there was a great social gulf between them. This gulf continued to widen during the eighteenth century. Between 80 and 90 per cent of bishops were nobles. Some of them, including Paris, Beauvais and Rheims, were peers of the realm; other bishoprics conferred upon their incumbents the title of prince, count or baron. The parish priests, on the other hand, were drawn from far less prestigious though by no means impoverished backgrounds, mostly in administration and commerce. Indeed, there is evidence to suggest that during the eighteenth century recruits to the parish clergy were drawn increasingly from rural areas rather than from urban élites, so that the social distance between the two orders of the clergy continued to widen.

There were also other than social tensions making for disputes within the first estate throughout the seventeenth and eighteenth centuries. In particular there was a protracted constitutional wrangle about the parts played by bishops and *curés* in the government of the church. The latter took a democratic view, maintaining their right to participate with the bishops in the running of the dioceses. In this they were supporting the ideas propounded by a seventeenth-century theologian, Edmond Richer. In the eighteenth century Richerism became enmeshed with Jansenism as the French bishops who were seeking to extirpate that proscribed doctrine, found themselves at odds with their clergy. With the approach of the Revolution the *curés'* demands became more outspoken, reflecting the growing divisiveness in the country. Their opposition culminated in the campaign linked with the drawing up of the grievance lists of 1789. Although this was a significant episode it also provides an example of how over-emphasis upon events immediately preceding 1789 may obscure the importance of longer-term historical developments.

Despite disagreements, the members of the first estate had many privileges and dignities in common. They could not be prosecuted in the secular courts, called up for military service, forced to billet royal troops or made to contribute money for their support. They enjoyed a number of financial exemptions including freedom from the chief direct tax, the *taille*. They also enjoyed social distinctions both collectively and as individuals: all priests could be immediately recognized by their long robe and tonsured hairstyle; bishops had in addition their staff and mitre, cardinals their red hat.

Finally, the importance of the first estate in French public life was recognized by its right to hold periodic assemblies where, besides making grants as a contribution to the king's financial needs, a valuable alternative for the clergy to regular taxation, it watched over the interests and privileges of its members and the religious life of the country. Thus it was able to intervene and make its views known to the king in all those sensitive political areas where great religious issues were at stake: the rights of the Gallican Church, the survival of Jansenism and Protestantism in France.

In the eighteenth century the privileged order of the first estate owned something like one-tenth of all the land in the kingdom. Its members occupied an important place at every level of society, from the humble country parish to the royal court itself; and politically the status of the first estate reflected the power of religion in France and justified the royal title of His Most Christian Majesty.

The second estate

The French nobility made up the second estate, and its relationship with the monarchy for a long time provided the key to the stability and survival of the old order. In return for its service to the crown, originally of a military kind, but later widened to include a host of administrative responsibilities, the king granted the nobility extensive rights and privileges which guaranteed its social, economic and political pre-eminence.

As within the first estate, there were substantial social divisions between the members of the second estate. At one extreme came the princes of the royal blood, the members of the king's own family, who were surrounded by the court nobility consisting of leading ministerial and ancient noble families who often performed honorary functions in the king's household or in that of one of the princes. At the other came impoverished provincial noblemen who were forced to labour in person on their land. Nevertheless, despite such enormous differences in status and wealth, membership of the noble order bestowed the same fundamental privileges on all. Some were honorific, like the right to wear a sword in public, to display a coat of arms, to take precedence in certain public ceremonies. Some again were judicial: the right to have their cases heard in a high court of law, to be exempt from corporal punishment, to be beheaded rather than hanged if found guilty of a capital offence. Others were financial: freedom from the *taille* and from the salt-tax, and although during the eighteenth century the nobility lost its total immunity from paying direct taxes, it invariably contributed at a lower than normal level of assessment. The most treasured possession of the second estate, however, until the second half of the eighteenth century, was its belief in the moral superiority of nobility: the virtues of generosity, honour and courage were seen as the distinguishing characteristics of the true nobleman.

How was this enviable status of nobility to be acquired? The only available channels were by birth or through the will of the king. A nobleman by birth automatically transmitted hereditary nobility to his children. Nobility, however, was only passed on in the male line so that the children of a noble woman who was married to a commoner would not acquire noble status. As for ennoblement by the king, this could take one of three forms. In return for a sum of money the king might bestow nobility upon a wealthy commoner. Louis XIV made clear his belief that, especially in times of military need, financial assistance to the state was worthy of such reward. This was not, however, a very common means of acquiring nobility and neither was the second method of ennoblement, admission to the Order of Saint-Louis in return for outstanding military service, a practice established in 1750 by Louis xv. By far the most common route to ennoblement was through the possession of certain offices, a procedure to which we need to devote some attention.

Certain administrative, judicial and financial offices bestowed immediate hereditary nobility upon their holders, while other offices gave personal nobility which became hereditary if maintained in the family for several generations. It is important to note that many of these offices could be bought, and thereafter, like any other form of property, could be bequeathed to the office-owner's heir. It has been estimated that in the eighteenth century alone between 30,000 and 50,000 people acquired nobility in this way, a sizeable proportion of the grand total of the second estate which was unlikely to have reached 400,000 by 1789. This indicates a significant fact about the French noble order, namely that although it formed a legally distinct and separate body in the state, it was not inaccessible to those with wealth and social ambition. Traditionally, aspiring commoners who had made their money in trade, worked their way up the legal or municipal hierarchy, or served in the household of a great nobleman, found their reward in the purchase of an ennobling office. Subsequently their children or grandchildren might marry into older noble families, particularly if the latter were in need of the financial support which the newcomers could provide. Thus sale of office, or venality, was an effective method of preventing dangerous social tensions from developing. It was also a means of recruiting into government service officials who were professionally trained for their work and, finally, it was a practice which brought much-needed money into the royal exchequer.

There was another side to the coin, however. Venality did arouse opposition within the second estate, from those of ancient lineage who found it difficult to accept that noble qualities could be purchased, and from those of limited resources who could not compete with the new men, especially when it came to buying commissions in the army. A military career was still viewed by some as the only fit profession for a nobleman. Yet while the old order survived these frictions could be absorbed. After all, the nobility was being constantly renewed. We have already observed the high proportion of new nobles recruited during the eighteenth century, and a similar story can be told about the earlier period. It has been possible to establish the ancestry of over 150 of Louis XIV's lieutenant generals, and we find that one in four of these high-ranking officers belonged to families which had only acquired noble status in the sixteenth or seventeenth century. Sale of office also limited the government's freedom of action, for officials who owned their offices could not be dismissed; and venality affected offices of great political importance, like those of Secretary of State and of the country's chief judges, as well as a wide range of lesser posts in the king's service. While it is true that ill-advised or oppressive royal policies could be more effectively resisted by an independent group of officials, so could necessary reforms. Nor was there any guarantee that all those who purchased office, or their heirs, would be efficient in exercising their responsibilities.

The most serious objection to the sale of office, however, was that it discouraged vigorous and enterprising merchants from continuing to contribute to the country's economic welfare. This was because noble status, which such people hoped to acquire, did not permit the making of money, in particular by means of trade and commerce. The ideal of 'living nobly' meant living off the rents of landed estates; depending on unearned income rather than on the profits of a business enterprise. Consequently, when rich and successful businessmen entered the second estate they had to give up their previous career, buy a suitable country property and live in the accepted noble fashion. This state of affairs was unsatisfactory for the government. It had to raise large sums of money in the form of taxation and therefore wished to stimulate economic activity. From 1669 nobles were permitted to involve themselves in maritime trade and from 1701 in wholesale trade. Later in the eighteenth century a small but significant group of business nobility emerged, who invested heavily in the coal mining and textile industries that were developing in the shadow of the Industrial Revolution in England. They were the exception, however, to the general rule that nobility should be identified with landed wealth. On the eve of the Revolution perhaps one per cent of the population was noble, and it owned between a quarter and a third of the land.

Despite internal divisions these property owners remained a formidable force united by shared privileges.

However, it would be misleading to suggest that this privileged group remained entirely opposed to reform and change. Louis XIV's attempts to restate the relationship between crown and nobility had a variety of consequences. One was that the increasingly impersonal nature of government, whatever the theoretical importance of the king's person, allowed power to shift into the hands of ministers, royal favourites, whose actions were arbitrary and whose authority was uncontrolled. Noble complaints grew against a regime of bureaucratic absolutism which took little account of meritorious service or the rule of law. Another consequence was the realization by a number of nobles, influenced by the ideas of the French Enlightenment, that service to the Nation rather than to the dynasty offered the second estate the best hope of political influence and authority. By the same token, however, the idea of universal service, implicit in the concept of the Nation, clashed with the idea of a society of orders which was defined in terms of inequality. During the final third of the eighteenth century nobles began to stress the importance of merit rather than heredity or worthiness in justifying their status. By 1789, when the noble estate constructed its grievances, the *cahiers de doléances*, it was prepared to contemplate a new regime, 'a society of free citizens, equal in law, subject to the same duties'.

The third estate

The vast majority of the French people, all those who did not enjoy the status of cleric or noble, found themselves in the third estate. Although this estate included almost every class and condition of person, ranging from the professors and doctors in the universities at the top level to the vagabonds and tramps of rural France at the bottom, we will concentrate here on two important groups only: the peasantry and the bourgeoisie.

The peasantry Over 80 per cent of the population worked on the land and perhaps about a quarter of all the land in France belonged to the peasants. A tiny minority among them were large-scale farmers and others owned enough land to provide their families with a living. But the majority, with little or no land, had to supplement their income by working for more prosperous neighbours. Forming the unprivileged base of society they were all subject to government taxes like the *taille*, and to unpaid labour service on the king's highways, the *corvée*. They also paid traditional dues to the clergy in the form of tithes, and to the local lord in rents and in kind. These permanent obligations left little spare cash for improvements. Nor was there any incentive to experiment since most lived too close to subsistence level to risk changing age-old ways. In this respect the conservative peasantry was at one with the nobles who were content to draw rents from their estates rather than exploit them for profit as English landowners were doing during the eighteenth century.

The bourgeoisie The word 'bourgeois' is usually translated as 'middle-class'. These days it implies a particular view of historical development associated with the writings of Karl Marx. In the eighteenth century, however, the word carried a far less precise meaning and applied to a variety of people. Essentially, however, it referred to those members of the third estate who resided in towns and made their living not by hard physical labour but by some kind of mental or artistic skill, or, if wealthy enough, through investment in land and government stocks. They might be doctors, lawyers or painters, middle- or lower-ranking office-holders (not all offices brought nobility to the purchaser), financiers involved in collecting royal revenue, or ship-owners from one of the great ports of Bordeaux, Nantes or Marseilles. There was no sense of class solidarity amongst this eighteenth-century bourgeoisie. Unlike the other two orders, the third estate had no clear identity, and these people were simply its most successful representatives who had discovered means of acquiring status and wealth beyond the normal expectations. They shared a common trading past for it was the commercial success of fathers or grandfathers which had provided them with the opportunity for advancement. That advancement, in imitation of the nobility, usually took the form of purchasing land. Indeed, it was with the leading bourgeois that the third estate came closest to the second. These were the men most likely to purchase nobility and thus satisfy the social ambition

13

first aroused generations earlier in the hearts of successful trading forebears. There was no fundamental hostility between the bourgeoisie and the nobility before the Revolution. Indeed, the nobility's tendency in the decades before 1789 to embrace the concept of merit underlined the growing community of outlook between the two groups.

3

Problems solved and unresolved: the eighteenth-century balance sheet

Finance and the economy

France was a country of great economic promise under the old order. It was a large fertile land with a population of some twenty million people in 1700, the highest in Europe. That population was to grow to twenty-six million by the end of the century. These figures make interesting comparison with those for England and Wales, for example, where the population rose from under six to nine million in the same period, or Spain, with an increase from seven and a half to ten and a half million. Yet the conservative attitudes towards the land which we have already discussed prevented its efficient exploitation and deprived landowners of much additional revenue. Money was not invested in land improvement and so agricultural productivity remained low. Yet there was plenty of money available, for after Louis XIV's death French colonial and European trade flourished as never before, bringing great wealth to merchant families, especially those operating from the western ports, like Bordeaux and Nantes. The problem was that for many merchants trade remained a means to an end. That end was entry to the second estate and the adoption of attitudes which were totally at odds with their former life-style.

This draining away of financial resources underlines the king's problem in squeezing adequate revenue out of the system in which those who had most wealth and the best opportunities for adding to it were largely exempt from royal taxation and disinclined to pursue capitalist ventures. The problem was becoming more serious as the cost of warfare rose. One of the chief obligations upon the monarch was that of defending his subjects against external oppression, and war was a common feature of European life. To enable the government to raise and equip professional armies adequate to fight long wars on many fronts, like that of the Spanish Succession (1702–13), financial resources were required far in excess of what could ordinarily be provided. Louis XIV had taken some emergency measures – the introduction of two new taxes, a Capitation in 1695 and a Tenth in 1710 – which had to be paid by privileged and unprivileged subjects alike. These were only temporary impositions however to meet the needs of war, and were not intended as a permanent solution to the government's financial dilemma. Yet they did breach the principle of the nobility's immunity from direct taxation at a time when one or two critics of this principle, including Louis XIV's great military engineer, Vauban, were beginning to advocate universal taxation. However, such opinions were very much in the minority and Louis's reign ended with the crown heavily in debt once more and lacking any acceptable alternative system.

When Louis XV succeeded his great-grandfather in 1715 he was only five years old, so, until the king reached his majority in 1723, the government was in the hands of a regent, Philip, Duke of Orléans. Orléans, who understood the need for drastic change, was attracted to the bold economic ideas of a Scotsman, John Law. Law established a state Bank of France, issuing bank notes which he hoped would reach into every corner of the country and stimulate economic activity. The bank was associated with a great national enterprise, a trading company in which all the subjects could invest and through which they could draw profits from the colonial riches which Law intended to exploit. The project required all elements of society to contribute to the common cause, and not to seek financial privileges and exemptions. It was a grandiose scheme owing much to the example of the Bank of England which had been established in 1694. Many Frenchmen were aware of the important part played by that institution in providing war funds for the anti-French alliance during the War of the Spanish Succession. But

Law's bank collapsed spectacularly in 1720, before his challenge to the privileged orders could be seriously mounted. The absolutism of the French political system made wealthy subjects dubious investors since, having no control over government policy, they could not protect their investment. In England, on the other hand, confidence in the bank sprang from investors' ability to influence policy via the House of Commons. Frenchmen turned to speculation, to a get-rich-quick approach which inevitably led to massive inflation, loss of confidence and a dramatic crash. At the end of the regency, therefore, the serious financial and taxation problems facing the government remained, although the stimulus which John Law had given to colonial trade continued to have its effect.

For the first twenty years of Louis XV's majority, government was in the hands of the king's former tutor, Cardinal Fleury, whose cautious foreign policy kept France out of expensive wars and serious debt. When he died in 1743, however, the country was already involved in a major European conflict, the War of the Austrian Succession which only ended in 1748. To help pay for it the controller-general of finance, Machault d'Arnouville, introduced a new tax in 1749 – the Twentieth – which was a 5 per cent levy on all incomes, whether derived from property, office or commerce, and was to apply irrespective of privilege. A fierce conflict ensued, in which the opposition was led by the general assembly of the clergy, as a result of which the first estate succeeded in gaining exemption from the tax. The opposition was particularly fierce since the tax had been introduced in peace time and therefore could not be defended on the grounds of a national emergency as the Capitation and the Tenth had been. Nevertheless the government introduced a second Twentieth at the beginning of the Seven Years War, in 1756, and a third in 1760, both to last for the duration of the war and to be paid by all the king's subjects except the clergy. The third Twentieth duly ended with the peace of Paris in 1763 though it was reintroduced between 1782 and 1786. The second Twentieth, like the first, remained a permanent levy.

The introduction of the Twentieths focuses attention on the dangerous tensions dividing government and society in France, tensions which were causing doubts to be expressed about traditional methods and values. First of all, a gulf existed between the government's 'modern' centralizing mechanisms and the archaic financial system which it had inherited. Government revenues came from 'ordinary' and 'extraordinary' measures, the latter usually a response to the greatly increased expenditure brought about by war. 'Ordinary' revenue consisted of direct and indirect taxes. Raising the former, the *taille*, was ultimately the responsibility of royal provincial officials, the intendants. Indirect taxes, including the *gabelle*, or salt-tax, as well as other levies on food and wine, were in the hands of tax-farmers. These were private operators who in return for annual payments to the crown were allowed to pocket whatever profits could be made from the collection of the various indirect taxes. The 'extraordinary' revenue consisted of government borrowing, either from wealthy financiers, or from individuals anxious to purchase financial or judicial office in order to climb the social ladder. This ramshackle system was further complicated by the fact that as new provinces had been added to the kingdom they had made their own financial agreements with the centre. The result was an even greater variety of taxes and exemptions and a network of internal customs barriers.

The justification for introducing the new bureaucratic machinery was that assured and adequate financial resources would thereby be made available for government as the level of its expenditure increased. Yet that could not happen until a degree of efficiency and rationality was introduced into the proceedings. It was not efficient to decide on the level of the *taille* without having any effective means of measuring what the country could afford; nor to entrust the collection of indirect taxes (and of direct taxes below the level of intendant) to people with a vested interest in profiting from their role. Neither was it rational to excuse the wealthy from paying direct taxation.

For a long time the government tried to make the best of a bad job. Hence the repeated re-introduction of the Twentieth, originally a temporary tax to be levied on all the king's subjects; and the intendants' attempts to collect taxes despite the barrier of long-held local liberties. The results of such efforts to introduce change surreptitiously were to encourage opposition and to stimulate radical ideas.

The opposition centred on the tradition of liberties which even the centralizing Louis XIV had acknowledged. As financial policy acquired a national perspective so it seemed to some that a national body, the Estates-General, should be convened to

18

consent to the financial demands of government and to oppose the arbitrariness of ministerial decree. This demand had become strident in the dark days of the War of the Spanish Succession, before Louis XIV's death, and it was renewed with the imposition of the Twentieth. It was linked to the emerging concept of the Nation whose wishes would presumably be transmitted to the king's government through the three estates meeting in conclave. Finally, as we have already seen, this national concept also added weight to the idea, already expressed by John Law during the Regency, that 'Immunities, privileges and exemptions must be regarded as abuses which cannot be abolished too soon. Clergymen, nobles or commoners, we are all equally the subjects of the same King; it is against the essence of being a subject to claim to be distinguished from the rest by the privilege of not paying tribute to the Prince. . . . Nothing is more important for the good order of a Kingdom than uniformity and it is to be wished that it may reign in the law and in taxation.'[3]

The government's desperate search for finance was therefore becoming ever more clearly linked with the need for fundamental changes in the social and economic structure of the country. When the disastrous Seven Years War ended in 1763 it was decided to experiment along lines suggested by the physiocrats. The physiocrats were a group of French economic writers who believed that agriculture was the key to the nation's wealth. They maintained that one means of stimulating agricultural production was by removing the controls, both within the country and at the frontiers, which prevented free trade in the vital commodity of grain. The theory was that this freedom would lead to a more vigorous economy and a large increase in the country's wealth. More money would then be available for payment in the form of royal taxes. However, the reality did not match the theory. Grain prices rose as those with a surplus to sell looked for the highest bidder. Outbreaks of public disorder followed, with accusations that the king was failing in his most basic obligation to preserve his subjects from starvation. The experiment was brought to an end in 1770.

This was not quite the end of physiocratic influence for at the very beginning of Louis XVI's reign, in 1775, Turgot, a friend of the physiocrats, was appointed controller-general of finance. He re-introduced free trade in grain but that decision coincided with a bad harvest and caused serious outbreaks of violence in

northern France, known as the Flour War. Turgot also planned to introduce a single tax on land, organized by means of representative assemblies of landowners, which would take the place of all the existing taxes. The opposition which these various proposals aroused led to his dismissal in 1776 but his successor, the Swiss banker Necker, was equally convinced that fundamental reform of the French tax structure could not be long delayed. However, he had first to face the additional problem of financing France's involvement in the War of American Independence, an adventure which was eagerly pursued by the government as a means of gaining revenge for French colonial losses to Britain in the Seven Years War. The war went well for France, but the financial cost was considerable. Historians, however, have recently begun to question the extent of Necker's responsibility for the financial crisis at the end of the old regime. In particular, his policy of raising loans, rather than increasing taxes, to cover the costs of the war, has been defended on the grounds that he had no alternative in the time available to him, and that the interest rate paid by the government on these loans, at about 6 per cent, though not cheap was by no mean ruinous. Necker hoped to make France more creditworthy, so that exceptional financial needs, like those created by war, could be met, as in Britain, by borrowing money rather than by the imposition of crippling new taxes. That was the objective behind his tax reforms but, like his Scottish predecessor, John Law, the Swiss banker had to work within a political system which did not inspire confidence in those with money to invest.

Part of the difficulty in allocating responsibility in this area arises from the unreliability of the surviving figures, though the situation was certainly deteriorating in the last decades of the *ancien régime*. It appears that at the end of the Seven Years War (1763) the government's financial deficit was some fifty million *livres*. That figure had been reduced to forty million by the time of Louis XVI's accession in 1774, but by 1786 it had reached one hundred and twelve million.

As well as the government's financial difficulties there was evidence in the 1780s of a deteriorating economy. Between the 1730s and 1770s France's increased population was absorbed without any threat to the country's political stability, for with harvests remaining generally good the cost of bread did not rise out of proportion to wages. However, the 1770s and 1780s were years dominated by poor harvests. French agriculture still depended heavily upon nature for the quantity and quality of its yield. It had not devised artificial methods of raising the level of productivity to take account of the additional mouths to feed, and to offset the unpredictable behaviour of the weather. As the amount of grain available to feed the enlarged population diminished, so its price rose; and there was no comparable rise in wages. A situation developed, therefore, in which the cost of basic food took up a large proportion of the total wage, leaving little or nothing for the purchase of other commodities. That in turn led to the decline of manufacturing industry, and those working in textiles in particular, whether in urban workshops or in the rural cottage industry, either became unemployed or had their incomes much reduced. In such an economic climate it was more difficult than ever for the government to raise the revenue that it needed unless it could finally persuade the wealthy privileged minority of the population to make a realistic contribution. It was against this ever more sombre background that the last attempt was made to reform the outdated financial relationships which plagued the old order. The attempt was made by Charles de Calonne who was appointed controller-general of finance in 1783.

Calonne's intention was to introduce a tax paid in kind, not in money, by all landowners irrespective of their status. This tax would replace the Twentieths, but, unlike those impositions, would be levied on clergy as well as laymen. It would not take the place of other direct taxes though they would be reduced. Internal customs barriers would be dismantled and once again free trade in grain would be introduced. None of these ideas was new nor were the difficulties faced by Calonne in attempting to persuade those most concerned, the landowners, to co-operate with him. His solution was to summon an Assembly of Notables. There were precedents for such meetings of lay and clerical dignitaries and it seemed to Calonne that in the tense days of the 1780s it was preferable to deal with the privileged groups alone rather than convene the three estates, meeting as the Estates-General, an event last witnessed in 1614. Besides, if the Notables could be persuaded to support Calonne's reforms, the third estate seemed unlikely to protest. In seeking to persuade the Notables,

Calonne re-introduced Turgot's proposal for a series of land-owners' assemblies, ranging from parish to provincial level.

The Assembly of Notables first met at the Palace of Versailles in February 1787. In April of the same year, in the absence of any significant progress, the king dismissed Calonne. The trouble was not simply the determination of the representatives of the privileged orders to hold on to their privileges, though that was partly the case with the clergy. By and large the notables accepted the fact that a radical shift in taxation policy was needed. However, they mistrusted the controller-general himself and the latter only heightened their suspicions by his inept handling of the delicate situation. Also Calonne represented a feature of royal government which, as we shall see in the next section, many found unacceptable. The cry for the reconvening of the Estates-General, which had last been heard in the 1770s, was taken up by the Notables and this time proved irresistible. By the time the estates assembled, in May 1789, the French government was once again facing a financial crisis with no sign of any long-term resolution of its problem.

Government

We have seen how royal government had prospered in France by guaranteeing a just regime, with respect for the rights and liberties of the various groups into which the subjects were divided. But we have also seen the difficulties into which the government was plunged when long-standing privileges acted as a barrier to effective action. Nowadays we might say that action was necessary 'in the national interest', but in the eighteenth century such an idea had only a limited meaning. The king had certain obligations. For instance he had to defend all his subjects against external aggression and therefore in times of war he could make demands upon them which would not be tolerated in peace time. Consequently, he could levy additional taxes on a temporary basis to help overcome a specific crisis. Normally, however, the king could not flout the laws and customs of the land which maintained the very unequal rights of his subjects without the risk of being accused of despotism. In a regime firmly based upon respect for the law such an accusation could prove very damaging to the stability of the country. Yet there was another side to the problem. As our discussion of the crown's financial difficulties has demonstrated, it was becoming impossible to run a 'modern' state on the basis of out-of-date views about the relationship between the government and the subjects. Here then was the dilemma facing the king and his ministers: how could they acquire more power without in the process undermining respect for the king's authority as upholder of the law?

It is now time to return to the question of the monarch's personal rule in the light of the changes which had been taking place for some time in the way in which royal government functioned. The growing complexity of international relations, the cost of maintaining large professional armies, and the need to extend central government control over the regions in the interests of internal security, all made it difficult for the monarch to rule in person. Although Louis XIV did maintain firm control over domestic and foreign affairs through his domination of and conscientious attendance at the royal council, even he had to pay increasing attention to the opinion of experts. By the end of his reign permanent officials were advising his ministers, and future ambassadors were being trained in the skills of diplomacy. In the provinces the all-purpose professional administrator, the intendant, represented the government. He was responsible for matters of public order and justice as well as finance, and was appointed to govern in one of the administrative sub-divisions of the country called a *généralité*. By the eighteenth century he had acquired a large staff of assistants and secretaries and impressive files of correspondence.

One result of these developments was a tendency for royal government to appear more concerned with administration than with justice, with efficient organization than with the legal rights of the subject. One clear indication of this shift may be seen in the declining political importance of the chancellor, the chief judicial officer in the state. His role in government was increasingly taken over by full-time administrators like the secretaries of state and the controller-general of finance. It seemed that the king was in the process of becoming the chief executive of the state rather than the guarantor of the old order. As the century progressed this impression was reinforced by the growing power of officialdom. For example, the royal council for finance met with diminishing frequency during the reign of

Louis XV (1715–74). Yet the number of financial decrees issued in those years bears no relation to the number of council meetings held, and it would appear that only one decree out of every eight or ten was promulgated after discussion in council, in accordance with the proper procedure. Most were issued not after consideration by the king and his councillors, but following discussions between the controller-general of finance and his permanent officials. That was certainly where the expertise was to be found, but once the direct involvement of the king and his council was removed from the process of governmental decision-making so was the legal justification for the form of government itself.

Neither Louis XV nor his grandson, Louis XVI, accepted that the nature of their authority had changed in any way. Although the eighteenth-century Enlightenment undermined belief in divine-right kingship, that belief remained part of the French royal tradition, as did the concept of legal kingship presiding over an unequal society of estates or orders. The kings' insistence upon this position actually put their authority more at risk by creating a credibility gap between the theory and practice of royal government. They were hopelessly torn between accepting the need and opportunity to use their agents in the centre and in the provinces to create a more efficient government machine, unchecked by outdated legal conventions and restraints; and seeking to reassure their critics that all the old values remained intact.

The most outspoken critics were the judges in the sovereign courts, the courts of appeal which were headed by the parlement of Paris. This source of criticism was to be expected since the registers of these courts, upon which their own judgements were based, all provided legal precedents in support of the traditional view. It must also be remembered that precisely because the king's political authority under the old order was seen as primarily judicial, so his courts of law had a political as well as a judicial significance. Their criticisms of the government had to be taken that much more seriously because these courts claimed to speak with the voice of legitimate French kingship which despotic administrators were seeking to overthrow.

However, in leading the opposition the parlement of Paris found itself in a position no less ambiguous than that of the crown. The language employed in the court's remonstrances, the

24

formal judicial supplications which it addressed to the king, implied a more radical stance than the judges intended. They seized upon the word 'nation' in order to suggest the existence of a political order in France, represented by the parlement itself, or by the Estates-General, which was independent of the crown. They increasingly employed words like 'citizen', 'society', 'humanity', 'the public' to encourage the notion of equality amongst the members of the Nation. Yet the essence of the parlement's authority lay in its conservative role as the defender of established laws and procedures, which required it to deny that the Nation could exist separately from the monarchy, and to confirm that the relationship between crown and subjects was by means of estates or orders. The court's remonstrances also reflected these traditional views to which most of the judges remained faithful. However, in seeking to lead the assault upon royal and ministerial despotism they risked giving support to new ideas, and new meanings to old words.

The sovereign courts were especially hostile to the government's tax-raising policies, notably after the outbreak of the Seven Years War in 1756, and their complaints came to a head in 1771 when the king authorized his chancellor, Maupeou, to exile the judges of the parlement of Paris and establish a new judicial body to take its place. Three other parlements, those of Rouen, Douai and Metz, were abolished, and the rest drastically reorganized. In particular, none of the new judges was allowed to buy his office. The system of venality had given his predecessors the independence to resist ministerial pressure, and Maupeou was intent on restricting that freedom. This was the government's most drastic move since the days of John Law in its efforts to gain greater freedom of action. It might have been the starting point for a fundamental reform of the whole political system, though that was unlikely since the king himself had no such ambitions. Indeed, Louis xv refused to abolish all the parlements, or to deprive them of their traditional political role. He was well aware that Maupeou's reform had encouraged the belief, already widely circulated by the parlements, that France was becoming a despotism. His successor had the same outlook and within a year of his accession Maupeou had been dismissed and the old judicial system restored.

Thus the scene was set for the government's final attempt

under Calonne to restore its fortunes, and to repel its critics. We have already seen that Calonne's efforts failed. At this point we might ask to what extent that failure reflected attitudes of and towards the controller-general himself. Calonne had made his reputation as an intendant and was associated therefore in the Notables' eyes with that 'ministerial despotism' which they detested. For he was empowered to override and supervise the decisions of all kinds of legally constituted local authorities, in the interests of the central government. Calonne was also known to be hostile to arguments of the parlements which would limit the powers of central government. He was one of the authors of a famous speech delivered by Louis xv in 1766 to the parlement of Paris in which such arguments were firmly rejected; and he had been a judge at the trial of the Breton magistrate, La Chalotais, a prominent critic of the government. It was not surprising, therefore, that he should have refused to involve the parlements in the proposals which he sent before the Assembly of Notables, though they would ultimately have to register whatever new laws emerged. After his dismissal and replacement by Loménie de Brienne the parlements, led by that of Paris, resumed their political activities.

The constitutional argument was becoming the courts' central theme. By the late 1780s the parlement of Paris was clearly asserting the Nation's independence from the monarchy and insisting, along with the Notables, that only the Nation's representatives, meeting in the Estates-General, could approve the sort of tax reform that Calonne and Loménie de Brienne were seeking. The king and his chief law-court embarked on a series of mutually destructive measures: the parlement was forced to approve Calonne's land tax, reintroduced by Loménie de Brienne, and its members were subsequently exiled *en masse* to the town of Troyes; they then rejected as invalid the enforced approval of the tax, and threatened to bring Calonne to trial.

By this time (August 1787) the magistrates of the parlement were receiving such support on the streets of the capital that one contemporary observer forecast civil war. The popular view was that the magistrates were opposing arbitrary government which, if not resisted, could impose heavier taxation at will. The parlement of Paris and the other provincial courts encouraged this view by emphasizing the need to restrict the government's power, not only in the field of taxation but more generally in the application of the law, including protection from arbitrary arrest and imprisonment. At length Louis XVI bowed before the pressure and summoned the Estates-General to meet in May 1789.

When the parlement of Paris assembled in September 1788 to discuss how the approaching meeting of the Estates-General should be conducted, the magistrates agreed that the voting procedure should follow the pattern of 1614, when the estates had last met. Counting would therefore be by estate and not by individual heads. In other words, the privileged first and second estates could always out-vote the third. At once the parlement lost its popularity with the people of the capital for it became suddenly clear that its concern was rather to prevent change than to champion their cause. The magistrates wanted a return to the old order in which legal rights and privileges would again be guaranteed against the arbitrary tendencies of government, a regime of unequal estates, not of individual rights. However, by this stage neither they nor anybody else could control the situation. The Estates-General duly met in May 1789. In June the third estate took over the title of National Assembly, and in July the Bastille was stormed.

War and international relations

France was fortunate to emerge from the War of the Spanish Succession (1702–13) with fewer losses than had seemed likely in the catastrophic middle years of that war. At the peace of Utrecht (1713–14) Louis XIV achieved his ambition of establishing his grandson on the Spanish throne as King Philip V, though on condition that the kingdoms of France and Spain should never be united under one ruler. Despite severe military defeats, at Blenheim (1704), Ramillies (1706), Oudenarde (1708), and, less damaging, Malplaquet (1709), France remained the strongest power in continental Europe. Overseas however, the loss of Nova Scotia and Newfoundland to Great Britain and the latter's acquisition from Spain of the Asiento, the exclusive right to supply black slaves to the Spanish Empire, suggested the beginning of a significant shift in favour of France's old enemy, Britain.

When Louis XIV died in 1715 French attention was not focused on the colonies but on Europe. Despite the ending of the war, Europe remained a very dangerous place, especially for a country bankrupted and exhausted. France was also about to be ruled by a regent, and past experience had shown that regencies were times of great political instability. France needed peace but still lacked security. The main problem concerned a number of disputed royal successions. Although Philip V had been forced in the interests of peace to renounce his claim to the French throne in favour of the new regent, Philip of Orléans (should the young king Louis XV die without heirs), he did not believe that his renunciation was valid. There was a real possibility, therefore, of a disputed succession in France. Similarly, Philip V's throne was still claimed by the Habsburg Emperor, Charles VI, who as the archduke Charles had been a candidate for it during the War of the Spanish Succession; while Philip was determined to regain Naples and Sardinia which were part of the Spanish Empire until 1700, but were acquired by the Emperor at Utrecht. Finally, the new King of England, George I, faced the threat of a Jacobite rising to restore the Stuarts.

The regent, who was much influenced in his foreign policy by his former tutor, the abbé Dubois, calculated that the best way forward for French diplomacy was to exploit the need and desire for peace felt by all the great powers after the protracted warfare of Louis XIV's reign. If Orléans could help to construct an international system of guarantees which would counter the fears of disputed successions around Europe, France and the regent himself, as a candidate for the French throne, would benefit. The Triple and Quadruple Alliances of 1717 and 1718 were the result of his efforts in this direction. By these treaties, France, Great Britain, Spain, the Emperor and the Dutch Republic all guaranteed the new succession arrangements first put forward at Utrecht. They also approved a complicated solution to the problem of the former Spanish lands in Italy. Naples and Sardinia were confirmed as imperial possessions, with the latter to be immediately exchanged for Sicily whose unfortunate ruler, the Duke of Savoy, had no alternative but to agree.

There are several significant points to be made about these

two treaties. First, they constitute a remarkable reversal of alliances which nobody could have predicted during Louis XIV's lifetime. France was now tied to all the chief members of the great coalition, Britain, the Emperor and the Dutch Republic, which had fought the late king almost continuously from 1689 to 1713. This unexpected flexibility in French foreign policy would have important repercussions over the following half-century. Surprisingly, France's natural ally by ties of blood, Spain, was least willing to accept the Quadruple Alliance and only defeat in a brief war with France (1719) persuaded her to do so. This leads us to the second significant aspect of these two treaties. Together they offer an early example of the principle of collective security in international relations. Great powers were beginning to co-operate in order to keep the peace. By guaranteeing each other's security they could impose a mutually acceptable settlement on smaller powers. Thus Spain was made to sign the Quadruple Alliance while the Duke of Savoy found himself at a stroke King of Sardinia instead of Sicily.

The Duke of Orléans contributed in two other respects to French security in Europe. Following the hostilities with Spain in 1719 he healed the rift by agreeing to a triple alliance between France, Spain and Great Britain in 1721. This reinforced the arrangements reached at Utrecht and in the Triple and Quadruple Alliances. The regent therefore succeeded in mending his quarrel with Philip V without reversing his previous policies, but he paid a price overseas for this increased security in Europe. To ensure Britain's signature, British traders were given considerable advantages over their French rivals in Spain's overseas empire. Finally, the regent had to take account of the Great Northern War which had broken out in 1700 and was to continue until 1721. Although the two chief adversaries were Sweden and Russia, George I was also concerned, not as King of Great Britain but as Elector of Hanover. Sweden was France's traditional ally in northern Europe and she was linked in a defensive alliance with Britain. However, Tsar Peter I was also actively seeking French support. Orléans' anxiety to secure the British alliance inclined him to support Sweden, though he did sign yet another triple alliance, in 1717, with Russia and Prussia, by which the two northern powers guaranteed their support for the peace of Utrecht. When the Northern War ended with the Treaty of Nystad (1721), brought about as a result of

French mediation, Orléans and Dubois began negotiations with Peter, but both Frenchmen died before a treaty could be signed. As a result, from 1726 Russia's fortunes became closely linked not with France, but with Austria.

France under Fleury

Cardinal Fleury, Louis xv's former tutor, was already in his seventy-fourth year when he became the king's chief minister in 1726, a position he retained until his death in 1743. Fleury was an astute and subtle diplomat who built successfully upon the regent's foreign policy. He held on to the British alliance, while the Emperor and Spain first resolved their differences (at the first treaty of Vienna in 1725), and then fell out again.

By this time a new factor, the Pragmatic Sanction, had become a significant element in international diplomacy. The Holy Roman Emperor, Charles vi, who had no sons, was anxious to bequeath all the Habsburg lands to his eldest daughter, Maria Theresa. As a first step he published in 1720 the Pragmatic Sanction, a document of Habsburg private family law which regulated the succession in Maria Theresa's favour. Having persuaded the various representative estates within his own domains to accept this new law he began the task of extracting acceptance from the European powers. After the death of the French regent, the Duke of Orléans, the Duke of Bourbon briefly became France's chief minister. He reversed the regent's policy of *rapprochement* with Spain. The Triple Alliance of 1721 between France, Britain and Spain had been intended to lead to a marriage between the young child, Maria Anna, daughter of the king of Spain, and King Louis xv. Bourbon decided instead that Louis should marry Maria, the daughter of a Polish noble-man, Stanislas Leszczynski, in the hope that she would shortly bear a son and thereby secure the French Succession. This decision led to the breaking off of diplomatic relations between France and Spain, and then to the signing of the first Treaty of Vienna between Spain and the Emperor whereby the former became the first European power to guarantee the Pragmatic Sanction. Subsequently relations between the two powers quickly deteriorated. However, as a result of Fleury's pacific policies the Preliminaries of Paris (1727) and the Convention of the Pardo (1728) once more committed France, Britain, the

Emperor, Spain and the Dutch Republic to the terms of the Quadruple Alliance of 1718. Then the pattern of foreign relations changed when in 1731 Britain's Prime Minister, Sir Robert Walpole, signed the second treaty of Vienna with the Emperor without consultation with his French ally. This action effectively ended an important period of Anglo-French co-operation during which the fragile peace of Europe had depended heavily upon that unlikely alliance.

Freed from his obligations to Britain, Fleury used his considerable diplomatic talents to restore French predominance in continental Europe. His opportunity came with the War of the Polish Succession in which France supported the claims of Louis XV's father-in-law, Stanislas Leszczynski, against Austrian and Russian support for Augustus III of Saxony. A Russian army installed Augustus on the Polish throne, but Fleury refrained from a serious military response. He was intent on maintaining British neutrality while he made the most of his opportunities at the conference table. By the third treaty of Vienna, signed in 1738 (though the war had ended three years earlier), Stanislas received compensation for the lost Polish throne in the shape of the dukedom of Lorraine which after his death would be incorporated into the French kingdom. Lorraine was the last of those key eastern and north-eastern frontier areas which were so vital to French security. Alsace, Franche-Comté and the three bishoprics of Metz, Toul and Verdun had all been acquired by Louis XIV. Only Lorraine eluded his grasp, but thanks to the old cardinal's diplomacy it too would become part of France in 1766. Fleury also ensured that the Emperor's influence in the Italian peninsula – and therefore the threat to French security – would be drastically reduced by the extension of the power of the Duke of Savoy in the North and the establishment in the South of the Spanish Bourbon kingdom of the Two Sicilies. In return for these considerable gains Fleury agreed to guarantee French support for the Pragmatic Sanction. By the end of the 1730s France's international standing was high; in 1739 it was French mediation that brought about peace at Belgrade between the Emperor and the Ottoman Turks.

Some of the developments of these years merit further consideration. When Walpole signed the second treaty of Vienna with the Emperor Charles VI, he guaranteed the Pragmatic Sanction. During the War of the Polish Succession the Habsburg

lands were obviously under attack and the Emperor expected
Britain to honour her treaty obligation and intervene on his
behalf. Walpole refused to do so, and relations between Vienna
and London were severely strained. Fleury, whose policy of
military restraint was designed to make it easier for Britain to
resist intervention, was encouraged to contemplate a reconcili-
ation between France and the Austrian Empire. While relations
between London and Vienna and London and Paris were becoming frosty, those between Paris and Madrid improved with the
signing of the Treaty of the Escorial, also known as the First
Family Compact, in 1733. Franco-Spanish co-operation brought
much closer the prospect of a colonial conflict between France
and Britain.

The War of the Austrian Succession and the Diplomatic Revolution

As Cardinal Fleury's powers waned, control over French foreign
policy passed to a group headed by the bellicose Count de Belle-
Isle, who favoured war against Austria. Their opportunity came
with the invasion of Silesia in 1740 by the new King of Prussia,
Frederick II. Silesia was part of the Habsburg empire which had
been inherited in that year by Maria Theresa, and its invasion
flouted Prussia's guarantee of the Pragmatic Sanction.

Early Prussian military success persuaded the French that
a Franco-Prussian alliance could lead to the partition of
the Austrian empire. They reckoned, however, without the
unpredictability and duplicity of the king of Prussia. In 1742
Frederick signed a unilateral peace with Maria Theresa, leaving
France to carry on the war against Austria in Italy, the Austrian
Netherlands, and the Rhineland. In Italy France enjoyed the
support of Don Carlos, the Spanish Bourbon ruler of Naples and
Sicily, and the Franco-Spanish alliance was further strengthened
in 1743 with the signing of the second Family Compact (the
treaty of Fontainebleau). When the war ended in 1748 the status
quo had not been disturbed: the Spanish Bourbons continued to
dominate the south of the peninsula and the Austrian Habsburgs
retained their control over most of the Milanese and Tuscany.
In the Rhineland the French found themselves pressed by Austria's ally, Britain, whose king, George II, was particularly
concerned with the security of his electorate of Hanover.

An Anglo-Hanoverian army marched east from the Austrian Netherlands to defeat a French army at Dettingen, in Bavaria, in 1743. However, France's military fortunes were restored by Marshal Saxe, the French commander, who won a succession of victories in the Austrian Netherlands, Fontenoy (1745), Rocoux (1746), and Lawfeld (1747). These successes gave France temporary control of the Austrian Netherlands, a valuable counter at the peace negotiations. The Treaty of Aix-la-Chapelle in 1748, which ended the War of the Austrian Succession, re-established the status quo in this region as in the Italian Peninsula. It was also restored finally outside Europe. For the War of the Austrian Succession was not only concerned with the ramifications of the Austro-Prussian conflict; it was also a chapter in the Franco-British struggle for world-wide colonial and trading hegemony. During this war France lost half of her warships and about one thousand merchant vessels. Britain's command of the sea also enabled her to deprive French ports of trade by means of naval blockade. Yet Britain was as anxious as France to make peace since the costs of maintaining her forces on a war footing and of subsidising her allies, were very high. Thus in India and Canada, as in Italy and north-western Europe, Aix-la-Chapelle dictated a return to the status quo. However, in terms of the quickening and momentous global struggle between France and Britain the treaty represented no more than a truce: hostilities would be resumed within a few years.

After 1748, with the support of Marshal Saxe, Cardinal Fleury's old peace policy towards Austria began to re-emerge in French diplomatic circles. France had become keenly aware of the military threat posed by Prussia and her untrustworthy ruler. Austria wanted a more reliable ally than Britain to help her regain Silesia. Britain for her part was looking increasingly to the approaching colonial struggle against France, and putting a new emphasis upon action overseas. France, a continental power with vulnerable land frontiers to defend, could not ignore the need for military support closer to home.

Negotiations between France and Austria proceeded slowly until the Convention of Westminster was signed in January 1756 between Great Britain and Prussia. News of this defensive agreement infuriated Louis XV whose ally Frederick was still supposed to be. France was persuaded to sign the first treaty of Versailles with Austria in May 1756. It too was a defensive agreement which the French believed would maintain the peace in Europe while the overseas war with Britain was fought out. In fact it provoked a Prussian attack on Austria via Saxony which resulted in the second Treaty of Versailles, an offensive alliance between France and Austria which committed the former to fight for the restoration of Silesia to Maria Theresa. Thus the Diplomatic Revolution was complete. The aim of a Franco-Austrian agreement had a history dating back to the Quadruple Alliance of 1718. Unfortunately for France its final accomplishment forced her to fight major wars on two fronts, in Europe and overseas. She had been out-manoeuvred diplomatically by Maria Theresa's chief negotiator, Count Kaunitz, at a time when French foreign policy lacked a dominant figure like Fleury to guide Louis XV's uncertain hand. It must also be noted, however, that those ideas of collective security, in terms of which the Franco-Austrian link was originally envisaged, had been destroyed by the polarization of Britain and France as overseas rivals, and by the unexpected emergence of Prussia as a formidable power in central Europe.

The Seven Years War and the War of American Independence

The war which ended in French humiliation at the Peace of Paris (1763) should not be viewed as a straightforward struggle between two great powers, Britain and France, each of them intent on world supremacy. In fact they had very different views of the world based upon considerations of geography and historical tradition. Viewed from the European stand-point, France was incomparably the stronger power because of her natural wealth in population and resources. She could equip and put large armies in the field to defend or extend her frontiers. Her social structure under an absolute monarch reflected that military priority, giving honour and privilege to those whose traditional role was to fight – the second estate – at the expense of merchants and traders. France had a considerable navy and a tradition of seamanship, which the British Prime Minister, the elder Pitt, hoped to destroy by depriving France of a share in the Newfoundland fisheries, but her security did not depend on her navy. Because she looked to the land rather than to the sea for that security her overseas territories were never the focus of attention of her government or subjects. From the standpoint of the wider world, therefore, France's resources and interest in her colonies failed to match Britain's. Her navy could not hinder the British navy from conveying and supplying British forces and preventing the transport and supply of French troops. France's involvement in a major war in Europe reduced her overall capacity to fight a maritime and colonial war, but even without war in Europe the problem of challenging Britain's naval supremacy would have remained. Where Prussia's role was crucial for Britain was in offsetting French gains in Hanover (still the electorate of the British king), which could then be used as a bargaining counter to regain lost territories overseas.

The gravity of the international situation persuaded Louis XV, in 1758, to appoint a new foreign minister, the Duke de Choiseul, whose talents in that capacity entitle him to rival Cardinal Fleury. Not that he could reverse the disastrous French losses overseas, but he used his professional diplomatic skill to acquire as satisfactory a peace settlement as France could have hoped for in the circumstances. Perhaps his greatest success was to tempt Spain into a new Family Compact (1761) which indirectly led to Pitt's resignation and a more flexible attitude by Britain at the negotiating table. Nevertheless, at the Peace of Paris France ceded Canada, a number of West Indian islands – Tobago, Grenada, St Vincent and Dominica – as well as some West African slave-trading stations, and all but a few trading stations of her Indian empire. Britain returned the profitable West Indian sugar islands of Martinique and Guadeloupe (as well as the smaller St Lucia), seized during the war, and the island of Goree off the North African coast, the centre for the traffic in slaves to the French West Indies. Significantly, since the French tended to view colonies in terms of narrowly commercial rather than political advantage, the restoration of these islands considerably softened the loss of the empty wastes of Canada. Nor did French seamen lose their right to fish off Newfoundland. Finally, the military conflict in Europe ended in stalemate and the restoration of the status quo.

The Peace of Paris remained, however, an intensely humiliating defeat for France. Even in Europe the combined power of France, Austria and Russia could not crush the upstart Prussians. There was no Marshal Saxe to lead France's armies, and until the appointment of Choiseul, no minister of distinction to guide her affairs. Yet the true explanation of the defeat is to be found less in personalities than in fundamental attitudes which, though they did not make French defeat inevitable, certainly made victory more difficult.

After 1763 Choiseul dreamt of revenge, and in preparation rebuilt the French navy and maintained France's restored alliance with Spain. However, he failed to keep Louis xv's confidence and was dismissed in 1770. The opportunity for revenge was presented to his successor, the Count de Vergennes, in the form of the War of American Independence which France joined in 1778. Her ally of the Family Compact, Spain, followed in 1779. On this occasion the British navy could not cope with the two Bourbon fleets acting together, and with the American rebels reinforced by French troops. Although France could not restore the situation to that existing before the outbreak of the Seven Years War, the Treaty of Versailles (1783) satisfied French honour. Britain lost her American colonies and France gained some compensation in Africa (Senegal) and the West Indies (Tobago). Yet France's financial state boded ill for the regime. Already after the Seven Years War 60 per cent of revenue was being eaten up in servicing the government's war debts. The American war added to the problem though perhaps not as dramatically as was once believed. Historians are still arguing about whether 'the price to be paid for American independence was a French revolution' (A.B. Cobban).[4]

4

France's cultural and intellectual influence

There can be no doubt that France was the cultural leader of Europe in the eighteenth century. French tutors and governesses found employment with noble families across the whole continent. French was the most commonly spoken language in educated society and the international language of diplomacy. Copies of Versailles were constructed by the kings of Russia and Prussia, Spain and Portugal, and by a host of minor Italian and German princes. French craftsmen in silver and gold travelled abroad to carry out commissions to French designs, and the Royal Academy of Sculpture and Painting in Paris provided the model for similar academies founded in Berlin and Vienna. Whatever the limitations of Louis XV as king of France, his court, presided over by the elegant Madame de Pompadour, set the tone for fashion and taste throughout Europe and provided the focus for one of the high points of European culture.

But the greatest impact upon the European mind was made by the writers of the French Enlightenment, that ill-assorted group of *philosophes*, as they were called, though they were publicists and propagandists as much as philosophers. What then were they publicizing? They were anxious to demonstrate that human reason was man's best guide in organizing society and government. During the seventeenth century scientific discoveries about the nature of man and the universe had begun to cast doubts upon the official view of church and state, which emphasized God's close involvement in human affairs and the overriding importance attached to seeking salvation in the next world. If by observation through the newly-invented telescopes and microscopes man could discover, for example, new stars in a universe of apparently infinite space, and acquire a new understanding of how the human body functioned, several revolutionary conclusions could be drawn. One was that by the exercise of their own reason human beings were capable of discovering the laws which governed their world, thereby removing God's direct role and threatening to eliminate Him altogether. A second was that mankind should concentrate on improving the quality of life in this world, by the application of common sense and intelligence, and should not allow the churches, supported by the secular powers, to impose their rules for eternal salvation which had often led to persecution and tyranny. Of course very few people drew such conclusions; even the great scientists themselves were devout Christians. But the propagandists of the French Enlightenment did crusade on precisely these lines.

Voltaire remains the best known of these writers. His literary output was prodigious: histories, plays, stories, letters, written over a long life (1694–1778), much of which was spent in exile from France. By the time of his death he was probably the most famous man in Europe. It is a measure of his world-wide reputation that in little more than half a century after his death thirty-four complete editions of his work were published. That figure is all the more impressive when the small size of the reading public and the limited opportunities for publicity are taken into account. During his lifetime Voltaire corresponded with the King of Prussia, Frederick II, and the Empress of Russia, Catherine II. He did not wish nor intend to undermine the authority of rulers, although he wanted them to use their power to benefit their subjects, by freeing them from the persecutions of the church and the legalized violence of the state, and by giving them the opportunity to enjoy material happiness and prosperity.

Voltaire's ideas are to be found scattered throughout his works, composed of an estimated 15 million words. However, the most important compendium of the ideas of the French Enlightenment is the great thirty-five volume *Encyclopaedia* (1751–86) edited by Denis Diderot. All the fundamental doctrines of the *philosophes* are to be found in this work, the importance of reason, the idea of human progress and the pursuit of happiness on earth. Religious toleration is defended and the power of organized religion attacked.

One of the contributors to the *Encyclopaedia* was Jean-Jacques Rousseau. Rousseau shared a number of enlightened attitudes, though his writings also reflect ideas to be developed in the early nineteenth century. He was a citizen of Geneva, not a Frenchman by birth, though he spent most of his life in France and is acknowledged as one of the outstanding figures of the French Enlightenment. He is also seen as one of its most radical and controversial thinkers whose hostility to monarchy and support for democratic government were seized upon by some of the French revolutionary leaders. He himself had no desire whatever to encourage revolution. His main concern was an old preoccupation of the Enlightenment: man's need to shape his environment in order to ensure his future well-being. Rousseau shared the hostility of the *philosophes* to the established churches and despotic government, as creating conditions unfavourable to man's development. Where he pursued an original line was in emphasizing man's moral rather than material welfare, and in suggesting that the state, which provided the environment for every citizen, should therefore have a moral role. The revolutionary possibilities of that idea could not have been seen even by Rousseau at the time of his death, the same year as Voltaire, in 1778.

It is not possible, of course, to be precise about the extent to which such ideas undermined the old order, though there can be no doubt that they did have some effect. By emphasizing mankind's ability to control its own destiny without divine support, and to live happily in this world without preoccupation with the next, the *philosophes* were challenging the king's role as God's lieutenant, and the church's role, supported by the state, as the sole and indispensable guide for every French man and woman. A belief in religious toleration and in the shared common sense of humanity threatened to undermine the inequalities inherent in the old regime. Yet none of these writers aimed at producing a revolution of the kind which occurred in 1789, years after their deaths. Indeed one of the greatest of them, Montesquieu (1689–1755), who stressed the sanctity of human law and custom in government, favoured greater authority for the nobility to prevent the king from becoming too powerful. What they all shared, however, was the ability to give powerful expression to ideas, attitudes and criticisms which had never before been set down in print. Rousseau in particular understood the potency of language and literature in confirming or challenging the social and political tenets of the established order; and his ideas were the dominating influence behind the literary works of radical revolutionaries like Fabre d'Eglantine. Whether ideas have any power to provoke revolution, except when used to highlight more practical discontents, is a question best left to the following, final section of this pamphlet.

5

The coming of the Revolution

We now return to the question raised in the introduction: whether the Revolution was caused by deep-seated problems or only resulted from circumstances arising shortly before 1789. It would in any case be a mistake to assume that historians could ever precisely account for a set of events as complex and unpredictable as those which made up the French Revolution. An unbridgeable gap must always remain between the sum of the causes listed by historians and the dramatic results produced, for it is not possible to take fully into consideration the countless rational and irrational actions of all the people involved. With that reservation in mind, however, it seems most likely that the Revolution broke out because long-term problems and resentments were brought to a head by events immediately preceding it.

We have already examined two of the areas in which deep-seated problems reached a critical point in the 1770s and 1780s, those of finance and government. In the former case, the financial stresses induced by the War of American Independence were made worse by the series of bad harvests which caused the price of bread to rise sharply. Behind both of these factors, however, lay the permanent problem posed by conservative social and political attitudes which prevented the rich land of France from yielding its true harvest and the government from acquiring necessary funds. By the spring of 1789 bread riots were sweeping the country, from Brittany in the north-west to Besançon in the east, from French Flanders down to Provence. Finally, in April, they reached Paris. There had been many examples of such rioting in the past, both in the capital and in the countryside, but they had not before led to revolution. The difference on this occasion seems to have been the accompanying political crisis which had already led the king to summon the Estates-General to meet in May 1789. The rioting took place while elections to this body were being organized, with the effect of raising hopes and expectations that at last something would be done to improve the conditions of those in need. By the time that the Bastille fell, on 14 July 1789, to another hungry Parisian mob seeking food and arms to defend itself against the king's troops encircling the capital, the Estates-General in Versailles had already transformed itself into a National Assembly: the Revolution had begun.

In matters of government too we have observed how the needs of efficiency and professionalism in royal officials had for a century clashed with the right to buy and inherit government offices, and with the various freedoms and privileges held by individuals and groups which could not be ignored without the king's administration being accused of despotism. Once again matters came to a head in the 1770s and 1780s, first with the short-lived reforms of the chancellor Maupeou, and then, following the failure of Calonne's reform programme, with the demands of the Assembly of Notables and in particular of the parlement of Paris for the calling of the Estates-General.

There is one other theme already discussed to which we might return at this point: the ideas of the French Enlightenment and especially the question of whether they played a part in the coming of the Revolution. Since they did not constitute a coherent programme for reform, and were not aimed at a particular group who might have been expected to carry them out, the answer must be, directly not at all. Yet over the period of the eighteenth century these ideas did raise doubts in the minds of educated people about the sanctity of the established order. Thus, when that order began to crumble, it was easier to find arguments to justify attacks upon divine-right monarchy, and to defend the earth-bound rights of man: liberty, property, security and resistance to oppression. But it must be emphasized that that only happened when the authorities had lost control of the situation.

So far it would appear that France's crisis in 1789 was political and depended crucially upon the government's failure to maintain credibility and effective control. That is a view taken by some historians, and in that context we must shortly try to assess the responsibility of France's kings, Louis XV and his grandson, Louis XVI. But many historians would not consider it adequate to explain the Revolution in political terms alone. They would insist upon the importance of long-standing social and economic factors. The Marxist view that the Revolution marked the rise of the middle classes at the expense of the nobility, though once generally accepted, is now no longer widely held. It has become clear that the rich bourgeois were property- and office-owners who invested in land in precisely the same way as the nobility did. Their wealth was not primarily capitalist, as Marxist ideology required; conversely, capitalist ventures in eighteenth-century France attracted a good deal of noble money. In other words, the wealthy bourgeoisie and the nobility shared the same economic outlook, while socially the former were regularly joining the ranks of the latter. However, it has also been suggested that advancement into the second estate was becoming more difficult for ambitious bourgeois of limited resources, owners of minor legal offices for example, than for prosperous merchants who could use their wealth to purchase instant nobility. As long as it remained possible for the first group to consider itself socially and economically *en route* towards the second estate, the irritation at being overtaken by monied upstarts could be contained. However, the decision of the parlement of Paris in September 1788 that the Estates-General should meet and vote by estate as in 1614 reminded these frustrated members of the middle class that there was a fundamental political distinction between their status and that of the noble order. Common economic and social attitudes developing in the course of the preceding century had helped to blur that distinction, but the summoning of the Estates-General brought it sharply into focus. For some bourgeois, therefore, the attainment of noble status suddenly became a remote possibility and with that realization their willingness to identify with the interests and outlook of the second estate came to an end. Long-term social and economic trends were thus diverted into new and dangerous channels by the events of 1788–9. Significantly, however, it was a political decision that signalled the shift.

Finally, we come to a consideration of the parts played by the last two rulers of *ancien régime* France, Louis XV and Louis XVI. Here we face a difficulty commonly met by historians, that of weighing the significance of an individual's contribution against the prevailing patterns of the age. It is not possible to ignore the actions and personalities of these two men, for the kingship which they in turn inherited was essential to the old order. Neither man was adequate for his task, though it might be argued that nobody else would have been either, for both were the victims of conflicting forces which appear to defy resolution without fundamental change of one sort or another. Louis XIV appeared to be more successful than his successors because he applied himself diligently and unremittingly to his duties as monarch. However, the dangerous implications for the crown of some of his achievements became increasingly apparent during the eighteenth century as the complexity of government and society increased.

Though Louis XV worked conscientiously at his task of ruling France during the first half of his reign he was easily bored. He lacked Louis XIV's dedication to the demands of his office and after the death of Cardinal Fleury (1743) he increasingly lost interest in government and sacrificed his popularity to the extravagance of his mistresses. He also appointed ministers with conflicting policies, hoping to maintain his own authority by exploiting the divisions between them. The result was government instability and the triumph of faction. Louis XVI also failed to give strong leadership, allowing ministerial rivalries to override commitment to long-term policies for reform, particularly in the areas of finance and the economy. His latest biographer challenges the conventional portrait of Louis XVI as stupid and lazy, arguing that the king's uncommunicative nature was to blame for this contemporary perception; though adding that his reputation for indecisiveness 'remains intact'.[5]

One result of the reigns of Louis XV and Louis XVI was that the royal office which they were expected to exercise in person and the whole system of government depending upon them, fell into disrepute and became ever more vulnerable to attack. Royal failures of will and character are not to be dismissed, therefore, though they are of only limited significance when weighed against the enormous pressures which eventually destroyed the *ancien régime*. Paradoxically, the kings' chief contribution to the crisis was their insistence that nothing had changed either in the personal nature of their authority or in their relations with their subjects. It was the fate of the French monarchy to be overthrown not because it had become despotic but because it had become irrelevant. Its last noteworthy political act, the summoning of the Estates-General, indicated that fact, and announced the Revolution.

Notes

1 J.M. Smith, '"Our Sovereign's Gaze": Kings, Nobles, State Formation in Seventeenth-Century France', *French Historical Studies*, 18(2), 1993, p. 415.
2 Nicholas Henshall, *The Myth of Absolutism: Change and Continuity in Early Modern European Monarchy* (London, 1992), p. 176.
3 Translated from a memorandum written in 1719 and published in P. Harsin (ed.), *John Law, œuvres complètes*, 3 vols (Paris, 1934), 3, pp. 39–61.
4 A.B. Cobban, *A History of Modern France, vol.1: 1715–1799* (London, 3rd edn., 1965), p. 122.
5 John Hardman, *Louis* XVI (London, 1993), p. 234.

Bibliography

Baker, K.M. (ed.) *The French Revolution and the Creation of Modern Political Culture*, vol. 1, *The Political Culture of the Old Regime* (Oxford, 1987)

Bosher, J.F. *French Finances, 1770–1795: from Business to Bureaucracy* (Cambridge, 1970)

Campbell, P.R. *The Ancien Régime in France* (Oxford, 1988)

Chaussinand-Nogaret, G. *The French Nobility in the Eighteenth Century: From Feudalism to Enlightenment* (transl. W. Doyle, Cambridge, 1985)

Cobban, A.B. *A History of Modern France, vol. 1: 1715–1799* (London, 3rd edn, 1965)

—— *In Search of Humanity* (London, 1960)

—— *The Social Interpretation of the French Revolution* (Cambridge, 1964)

Darnton, R. *The Literary Underground of the Old Regime* (London, 1982)

Doyle, William *Origins of the French Revolution* (Oxford, 1980)

—— *The Ancien Régime* (London, 1986)

Echeverria, D. *The Maupeou Revolution: a Study in the History of Libertarianism: France, 1770–1774* (Baton Rouge, 1985)

Egret, J. *The French Revolution, 1787–88* (transl. W.D. Camp, Chicago, 1977)

Ford, F.L. *Robe and Sword: the Regrouping of the French Aristocracy after Louis XIV* (Cambridge, Mass., 1953)

Hardman, John *Louis XVI* (London, 1993)

Harris, Robert D. *Necker: Reform Statesman of the Ancien Régime* (Berkeley, 1979)

Harsin, P. (ed.) *John Law, œuvres complètes* 3 vols (Paris, 1934)

Henshall, Nicholas *The Myth of Absolutism: Change and Continuity in Early Modern European Monarchy* (London, 1992)

Johnson, Douglas (ed.) *French Society and the Revolution* (Cambridge, 1976)

Kley, D. van *The Damiens Affair and the Unravelling of the Ancien Régime, 1750–1770* (Princeton, 1984)

Lucas, Colin (ed.) *The French Revolution and the Creation of Modern Political Culture*, vol. 2, *The Political Culture of the French Revolution* (Oxford, 1988)

Mousnier, Roland *The Institutions of France under the Absolute Monarchy, 1598–1789*, vol. 1 (transl. B. Pearse, Chicago, 1979), vol. 2 (transl. A. Goldhammer, Chicago, 1984)

Riley, James C. *The Seven Years War and the Old Regime in France: the Economic and Financial Toll* (Princeton, 1986)

Shennan, J.H. 'Louis XV, public and private worlds', in A.G. Dickens (ed.), *The Courts of Europe* (London, 1977)

—— *Philippe, Duke of Orléans, Regent of France, 1715–23* (London, 1979)

—— *International Relations in Europe, 1689–1789* (London, 1995)

Smith, J.M. '"Our Sovereign's Gaze": Kings, Nobles, State Formation in Seventeenth-Century France', *French Historical Studies*, 18(2) (1993)

Stone, Bailey *The Genesis of the French Revolution: A Global Historical Interpretation* (Cambridge, 1994)

Taylor, George V. 'Non-capitalist Wealth and the Origins of the French Revolution', *American Historical Review*, vol. 72 (1967)

Temple, Nora *The Road to 1789: From Reform to Revolution in France* (Cardiff, 1992)

White, R.J. *The Anti-Philosophers* (London, 1970)